Silver jewelry

Silver

Peter Murray

A⁺

Smart Apple Media

COPYRIGHT

✿ Published by Smart Apple Media

1980 Lookout Drive, North Mankato, MN 56003

Designed by Rita Marshall

Copyright © 2002 Smart Apple Media. International copyright reserved in

all countries. No part of this book may be reproduced in any form without

written permission from the publisher.

Printed in the United States of America

✿ Photographs by Pat Berrett, JLM Visuals (Richard Jacobs), Wolfgang

Kaehler, Tom Myers, Tom Stack & Associates (Brian Parker, Tess & David

Young)

✿ Library of Congress Cataloging-in-Publication Data

Murray, Peter. Silver / by Peter Murray. p. cm. − (From the earth)

Includes index.

✿ ISBN 1-58340-109-1

1. Silver−Juvenile literature. [1. Silver.] I. Title. II. Series.

TN761.6 .M874 2001   669.23−dc21   00-068794

✿ First Edition 9 8 7 6 5 4 3 2 1

Silver

C O N T E N T S

Ancient Uses of Silver

How are mirrors like dental fillings? What do photographers and rainmakers both need to do their work? What do batteries, jewelry, printed circuits, and old coins have in common? ❂ Each one of them uses silver, one of our most valuable metals. ❂ Like gold and copper, silver is one of the few metals that can be found in its pure, or "native," form. Ten thousand years ago, Stone-Age humans pounded and shaped nuggets of native silver into jewelry and other

Silver in its pure form is quite soft

decorative objects. ☀ Around 2500 B.C., early metalworkers

learned to extract silver from **ore**. As silver became easier to

mine and refine, people began to use pieces of silver as money.

Around 700 B.C., these pieces were shaped **United States dimes and quarters made before 1965 are 90 percent silver.**

into round, flat disks. Each disk, or "coin," had

a certain value. By 500 B.C., silver coins were

used as money in Greece, China, and Asia

Minor. Silver coins were common until the 1960s, when

most countries stopped using them.

An ancient silver coin

The Properties of Silver

Silver is a soft, heavy, white metallic **element**. It is the best natural conductor of heat and electricity. It reflects light better than any other metal, which makes it a good coating for mirrors. ☼ Pure silver is too soft for many uses. Jewelry and silverware are usually made of 92.5 percent silver and 7.5 percent copper. This silver-copper **alloy**, called sterling silver, is very hard and durable.

"Tarnished" silverware is coated with a thin layer of silver sulfide.

Tea sets are often made of silver

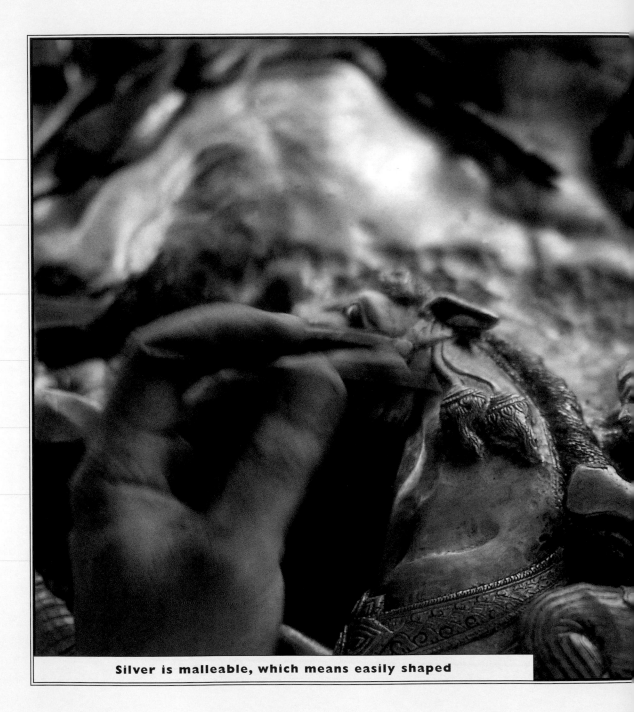

Silver is malleable, which means easily shaped

Silver Mining

In 1859, near what is now Virginia City, Nevada, prospectors searching for gold noticed a sticky, gray-blue mud clinging to their picks and shovels. To their surprise, they had discovered the largest silver **lode** in history! ☀ Named the Comstock Lode, the ore deposit turned out to be six miles (9.6 km) long and worth more than 300 million dollars. The area is still mined today, although the richest ore is gone. ☀ Today, most silver comes from Mexico,

The Comstock Lode was named after Henry Comstock, the prospector who discovered it.

Canada, Australia, and the United States. Silver is an important

by-product of copper mining. With modern mining methods,

silver can even be extracted from low-grade ores.

Silver ore is a mixture of metal and rock

Silver Today

When you look at yourself in a photograph or mirror, you are seeing silver. ☀ More than a third of all the silver mined today is used for photography. Camera film has a thin coating of a light-sensitive silver **compound**. When the shutter on the camera opens and closes, light hits the silver coating, causing chemical changes. When the film is developed, the silver compound darkens where the light hit it. This is how photographic negatives are made. To make a photograph,

A silver mine in Nevada

light is shined through the negative onto paper coated with

another silver compound. Again, the silver compound darkens

where the light hits it, and the result is a **Airplanes may drop silver iodide crystals into clouds to make them drop their rain.**

photograph. ☀ The second most common

use of silver is for making mirrors. Pure

silver is highly reflective. When a piece of

glass is coated with a thin film of silver, it reflects light.

That is how mirrors are made. ☀ Silver is also used for

jewelry, dental fillings, batteries, coins, electrical connectors,

Silver has many industrial uses

19

photocells, and printed circuits used for computers and other electronic devices. One of the most common uses is for fine silverware and silver plating because of silver's sparkle, its ability to be easily shaped, and its bacteria-killing properties.

☀ Whether we are eating an apple with silver fillings in our teeth, using a computer, taking a photo, or looking in the mirror, silver is a part of our lives.

A silversmith is a worker who shapes silver

How to Make Silver Sulfide

What You Need

A hard-boiled egg

A silver dime or quarter with a date 1964 or older (coins made after 1964 are not real silver)

Silver polish or tarnish remover

A small box or jar

What You Do

1. Polish the silver coin with the silver polish or tarnish remover. The coin must be very clean and shiny.
2. Put the clean coin in the box or jar.
3. Cut the hard-boiled egg in half and crumble the egg yolk over the coin. Wait one week, then look at the coin.

What You See

After one week, the coin will have turned dark, or tarnished. Hydrogen sulfide from the egg yolk (the stuff that makes that "rotten egg" smell) combines with the silver to make silver sulfide, the black film on the coin.

American coins were once made of silver

INFORMATION

Index

Words to Know

alloy (AL-oy)—a mixture of two metals

compound (COM-pound)—a combination of two or more elements

element (EL-e-ment)—a pure substance that cannot be broken down chemically; silver, sulfer, and oxygen are examples of elements

lode (LODE)—a rich mineral deposit

ore (OR)—a mixture of rock and metal

silver iodide (SIL-vur EYE-o-dyed)—a compound of silver and iodine used for photography and seeding clouds

Read More

Knapp, Brian. *Copper, Silver and Gold*. Danbury, Conn.: Grolier Educational, 1996.

Otfinoski, Steve. *Coin Collecting for Kids*. Norwalk, Conn.: Innovative Kids, 2000.

Symes, R. F. *Rocks and Minerals*. New York: Knopf, 1988.

Internet Sites

Ask-a-Geologist

http://walrus.wr.usgs.gov/docs/ask-a-ge.html/

The National Mining Hall of Fame and Museum

http://www.leadville.com/miningmuseum

American Museum of Natural History

http://www.amnh.org